ISBN 978-0-656-59265-4
PIBN 11288088

English
Français
Deutsche
Italiano
Español
Português

www.forgottenbooks.com

Mythology Photography **Fiction**
Fishing Christianity **Art** Cooking
Essays Buddhism Freemasonry
Medicine **Biology** Music **Ancient
Egypt** Evolution Carpentry Physics
Dance Geology **Mathematics** Fitness
Shakespeare **Folklore** Yoga Marketing
Confidence Immortality Biographies
Poetry **Psychology** Witchcraft
Electronics Chemistry History **Law**
Accounting **Philosophy** Anthropology
Alchemy Drama Quantum Mechanics
Atheism Sexual Health **Ancient History**
Entrepreneurship Languages Sport
Paleontology Needlework Islam
Metaphysics Investment Archaeology
Parenting Statistics Criminology
Motivational

Mary J. Huntington

Vol. IX   September, 1926   No. 5

BULLETIN

Sweet Briar College

6142   SWEET BRIAR, VIRGINIA

LETTER TO STUDENTS

STUDENTS REGISTERED
1926-1927

Published by Sweet Briar College

Sweet Briar, Virginia

NOVEMBER—JANUARY—APRIL—JUNE—JULY—AUGUST—
SEPTEMBER

ntered as second-class matter at the post-office, Sweet Briar, Virginia

LETTER TO STUDENTS

To the Students Entering Sweet Briar:

As President of Sweet Briar College it is I who claim the privilege of being the first to welcome you to its opportunities, its beauties and its obligations. To the students who have already been at Sweet Briar I say simply, "Welcome home to what we intend to make the best and happiest year yet spent at college." If this intention is realized, to the students coming for the first time I offer congratulations on their opening year and urge an ambition to get the best that is there.

Sweet Briar is beautiful and the daily life a bit enchanting with a very direct and simple appeal, but our business is mental and spiritual growth. The student will enjoy the life most who pursues it with an eager mind for new light on the true and the eternal, and who so intelligently manages herself and her time as to keep this in the first place.

One of the cherished ideals of Sweet Briar is the belief that college women are capable of governing themselves and the students are trusted to maintain their own discipline. The honor system prevails, and there is no more valuable acquisition to be gained at college than an understanding of it and a scrupulous self-discipline under it. The President, the Dean and the Faculty stand ready at all times for advice and assistance. Each Freshman has a faculty adviser who will guide and direct her in her work, and in addition a student associate from the upper classes who will aid her to understand the social and student traditions and the real spirit of Sweet Briar. The Freshman class, as a whole, has a general adviser, Miss Mary Searle, who is accessible at all times.

Let me especially urge the Freshmen to arrive in time to be ready for the carefully planned opening program for Freshmen on Tues-

(1)

day morning. The Freshmen halls will be ready for students on Monday September 20th.

Ave atque vale I say, with expectant eyes aimed only to the future.

Faithfully yours,

META GLASS

STUDENTS REGISTERED

Session 1926-1927

Name	*Address*	*Roommate*

Abernethy, Margaret J., 123 W. Smith St., Greensboro, N. C........A. W. Smith

Ailes, Serena, 620 Virginia Park, Detroit, Mich,..............................L. Prentis

Albers, Eleanor S., 900 N. 12th St., Ft. Smith, Ark.....M. Leigh, E. B. Mathews

Alsop, Camilla P., 1832 Monument Ave., Richmond, Va.....................E. Ervin

Ambrose, Martha, 958 S. Willetta St., Memphis, Tenn.............R. Lowrance

Anderson, Evelyn M., 420 St. Marks Ave., Westfield, N. J.....A. Patton,
> M. Chaffee

Antrim, Nora L., 2028 Monument Ave., Richmond, Va............A. Gochnauer

Armstrong, Mary E., 1025 5th Ave., Huntington, W. Va.

Ashhurst, Anne C., University, Va........E. Councill, M. Montague, E. Clement

Atkinson, Teresa, W., 916 Peachtree St., Atlanta, Ga...............S. de Saussure

Aunspaugh, Ruth, Box 780, Raleigh, N. C...................M. Cramer, M. Close

Babbitt, Alice D., 3333 No. Charles St., Baltimore, Md........M. F. Green

Bachman, Elizabeth G., 29 Melrose Pl., Montclair, N. J...E. Miller, H.Harpster

Bailey, Pauline J., Mabscott, W. Va.

Baker, Emma F., Aberdeen, Md..............................E. Guigon, M. Shelton

Baker, Jette L., 2140 Rivermont Ave., Lynchburg, Va....................N. Royer

Ballard, Evelyn T., 1412 Quarrier St., Charleston, W. Va........E. P. Phillips

Barber, Alice C., 439 N. Lake St., Aurora, Ill.................................P. Gates

Barksdale, Telia B., 1034 Graydon Ave., Norfolk, Va............A. Musgrave

Barnett, Frances W., 95 E. 14th St., Atlanta, Ga............................S. Buckley

Bartels, Gertrude, 1625 Vinton Ave., Memphis, Tenn............C. Thompson

Beard, Helen H., Amherst, Va.

Bean, Mary A., Wayside Pl., University, Va...............................M. Bemiss

Beeson, Adaline R., Farmington, W. Va.

Bemiss, Maria S., Richmond Trust Co., Richmond, Va...............M. A. Bean

Benton, Athlein B., Fremont, N. C.   ....E. Braswell

Berger, Rose A., Falmouth, Ky.

Bernard, Mary R., 224 Fillmore St., Petersburg, Va........................C. Straus

Bird, Caroline Page, 41 Uni. Pl., University, Va........................A. B. Price

Blake, Alice, 1016 Sherman Ave., Madison, Wis........................M. Gressitt

Blake, Anna K., 116 Stacy Ave., Trenton, N. J.............................B. Burgess

Blake, Ellen W., 839 Redgate Ave., Norfolk, Va.................H. Weitzmann

Boone, Arline R., 307 Mahantongo St., Pottsville, Pa.

Boone, Elizabeth H., 914 Mahantongo St., Pottsville, Pa.........M. Murphey

Boone, Jeanette, 914 Mahantongo St., Pottsville, Pa....................E. Gilchrist

Bortz, Dorothy, Sunnyslope, Uniontown, Pa.

Boynton, Laura B., Waco, Texas.

Braswell, Emily H., 226 Sunset Ave., Rocky Mount, N. C............A. Benton

Brent, Anne M., 444 S. 2nd St., Lexington, Ky........C. Stanbrough, E. Duvall

Brightbill, Katherine M., 32 W. Main St., Hummelstown, Pa.

Bristol, C. Louise, 181 Buffalo St., Warsaw, N. Y................................E. Jones

Brockenbrough, Belle, 607 No. 6th St., Lafayette, Ind.

Bromfield, Marion S., Brevard, N. C...M. Sanford

Bronough, Mildred P., Northport, N. Y...B. Lewis

Brooke, Sue H., 2215 Monument Ave., Richmond, Va...................M. Neal

Brown, Charlotte H., 1601 5th Ave., Huntington, W. Va.................B. Metz

Brown, Flo G., 1601 5th Ave., Huntington, W. Va...............M. A. Hughes

Brown, Janie R., 35 Beardon Ave., Ashville, N. C........................K. Wilson

Brown, Katherine E., 26 No.Seminole Rd., Jacksonville, Fla........E. H. Bryan

Brown, Madeline E., Alumni Ave., Hopkinsville, Ky........E. Quisenberry,

                                   J. Snowdon, K. Owens

Brown, Nedra, 45 Lenox Rd., Summit, N. J................................V. Chaffee

Bruce, Eleanor, 503-8th & Elm Sts., Orange, Tex.....................H. Mathews

Bruce, Janet W., 37 Gesner Ave., Nyack, N. Y...........................J. Wilkinson

Bryan, Elizabeth H., 44 Avondale Circle, Jacksonville, Fla............K. Brown

Bryan, Elizabeth R. P., 118 Park Drive, Charlotte, N. C.

Buckley, Sara, 621-8th St., Laurel, Miss.....................................F. Barnett

Bunting, Daphne B., 500 W. 122 St., New York City...E. Jones, E. Dickinson

Bunting, Dorothy, 500 W. 122 St.,New York City.

Burgess, Betsey, Huntington, L. I...A. K. Blake

Burks, Lucille, 1218 So. 3rd St., Louisville, Ky...............................M. Lee

Burks, Mary L., Amherst, Virginia

Bushey, Mildred P., 247 Hummel Ave., Lemoyne, Pa...................A. K. Close

Callison, Sara E., 509 N. 7th St., Lafayette, Ind.

Callison, V. Jane, 509 N. 7th St., Lafayette, Ind....................M. Kindleberger

Campbell, Virginia L., 103 E. 86 St., New York City............................L. Lutz

Cannady, Mary F., Amherst, Va.

Carnes, N. Elizabeth, 3117 Barcelona Ave., Tampa, Fla...............A. Lokey

Carpenter, Margaret H., 3302 Chadbourne Rd., Cleveland, O........M. Sturges

Cates, Elizabeth, 123 Advent St., Spartanburg, S. C.....R. Manning, E. Forsyth

Cather, Elizabeth A., 2908 Gaines St., Little Rock, Ark...........E. Nichols

Chaffee, Marian K., 395 Swarthmore Ave., Swarthmore, Pa...................
                A. Patton, E. Anderson

Chaffee, Virginia L., 395 Swarthmore Ave., Swarthmore, Pa............N. Brown

Chambers, Delma A., 4205 Maine Ave., Baltimore, Md............M. Oakford

Chapman, Louise, Audubon Park, Louisville, Ky.........................K. Whaley

Clark, Eleanor E., 7003 Euclid Ave., Cleveland, O............K. Marr

Clark, Mary F., 116 S. Wade Ave., Washington, Pa...............E. Orr

Clausen, Catherine H., 2330 Harrison St., Davenport, Iowa.....M. C.Woodworth

Claybrook, Evelyn L., 750 Washington St., Cumberland, Md.

Clement, Elizabeth C., Chatham, Va.........A. Ashurst, E. Councill, M. Montague

Close, Anna K., 5700 Wellesley Ave., Pittsburgh, Pa...................M. Bushey

Close, Mary E., 5700 Wellesley Ave, Pittsburgh, Pa.....M. Cramer, R. Aunspaugh

Cloud, Pauline A., Hamlet, N. C.

Coe, Kate T., 50 James St., Englewood, N. J...............................E. Hibbs

Coles, Charlotte L., 222 W. Franklin St., Troy, O.........................V. Dail

Collins, R. Louise, 200 Boulevard, Summit, N. J............................E. Luck

Compton, Caroline R., 2408 Drummond St., Vicksburg, Miss.

Conaghan, Dorothy A., 2307 Arleigh Drive, Cleveland, O............J. Halsey

Conklin, Louise A., Green Hill Rd., Madison, N. J.*...........................
           E. Kohn, E. Prescott, A. Newell

Conway, Anne F., Danville, Va...S. Davidson

Conway, Charlotte, E., Danville, Va. ....F. Coyner

Copeland, Elizabeth R., 5316 Huntington Ave., Newport News, Va..F. Gray

Copeland, Mary C., 444 N. Maple Ave., Greensburg, Pa............G. Ferguson

Cottman, Frances J., 107 S. Beech St., Casper, Wyo.......................K. Ryan

Councill, Elizabeth A., Hickory, N. C. A. Ashurst, M. Montague E. Clement

Cox, Elizabeth P., 2100 Confederate Pl., Louisville, Ky...............J. Gall

Coyner, Frances E., Marion, Va..C. Conway

Cramer, Margaret C., 2596 Fairmount Blvd., Cleveland, O......M. Close,
                  R. Aunspaugh

Crane, Elizabeth P., 209 Central Ave., Cranford, N. J...................H. Davis

Cravens, Elizabeth, 2200 Douglas Blvd., Louisville, Ky..............L. Dailey

Crenshaw, Elizabeth, 1301 Agnes Pl., Memphis, Tenn...............C. Giesecke

Crews, Elizabeth, 207 Rutledge St., Spartanburg, S. C............S. Dodgen
       D. Fowler, M. Timmerman, E. Ferguson

Crockett, Virginia L., Ardmore. Okla.

Cucullu, Margaret A., 109 Madison St., Lynchburg, Va.........M. L. Shepherd

Culver, Mary V., 5039 Walnut St., Philadelphia, Pa.................D. Meginniss

Cumnock, Eva A., Van Rensselaer Ave., Stamford, Conn............M. Macqueen

Curtis, Merry S., 606 S. 11th St., Lafayette, Ind....................A. Johnstone

Dail, Virginia, 202 Greendale Ave., Cincinnati, O.........................C. Coles

Dailey, Louise W., 329 Stoner Ave., Paris, Ky............................E. Cravens

Daily, Mary B., Owingsville, Ky...C. B. Williams

Dance, Sarah E., 714 Jackson St., Corinth, Miss....................A. H. Shepherd

Darrow, Dorothy, 104 Field Point Rd., Greenwich, Conn.

Davidson, Serena B., 102 So. Battery, Charleston, S. C...............A. Conway

Davies, Virginia D., Clifton Forge, Va.   E. Hurlock

Davis, Dorothy J., 28 E. 34th St., Bayonne, N. J.

Davis, Helen M., 1128—4th Ave., Rock Island, Ill.........................E. Crane

de Saussure, Sarah C., 30 Park Drive, Atlanta, Ga.........................T. Atkinson

Dey, Virginia B., 509 Westover Ave., Norfolk, Va.....................M. Pleasants

Diack, Margaret G., 744 Bellefonte Ave., Lock Haven, Pa.................M. Hall

Dickinson, Esther G., 366 Sanford Ave., Flushing, N. Y...E. Jones, D. Bunting

Dillard, Elizabeth M., 408 Summit St., Winston-Salem, N. C.....E.Wilkinson

Dillon, Jane, Piedmont Rd., Atlanta, Ga....................................N. Moffett

Dodgen, Sarah K., 157 Pine St., Spartanburg, S. C.....E. Crews, D. Fowler

                                                      M. Timmerman, E. Ferguson

Doyle, Suzanne, 440 Bank St., Beaver, Pa.....................................E. B. Kumm

Dunlap, Harriet S., 614 Orleans Ave., Keokuk, Iowa.

Dunlap, Sophia W., 2203 S. Georgia Ave., Mobile, Ala............R. Faulkner

Duvall, Eleanor H., Cheraw, S. C............................C. Stanbrough, A. Brent

Earle, Mary C., 308 E. North St., Greenville, S. C...............M. Lawrence

Eaton, Margaret S., 308 East Beach, Gulfport, Miss................S. von Schilling

Edmands, E. Evaline, 957 Williams Blvd., Springfield, Ill.............F. Reed

Edmondson, Margaret L., Route No. 1, Clarksville, Tenn............L. Fishburne

Eldridge, Katharine I., B-6 Calvert Court, Baltimore, Md............E. Riely

Ellis, Clarisse, 607-2nd Ave., Salt Lake City, Utah...M. K. Robbins, D. Wyckoff

Emery, Katharine D., 305 Park St., Montclair, N. J.

Ervin, Elinor M., Spring Hill P. O., Mobile, Ala........................C. Alsop

Eskesen, Alice M., 155 N. Euclid Ave., Westfield, N. J.....D. Garland,

                                                      M. B. Green

Everett, Sarah C., Selwyn Ave., Myers Park. Charlotte, N. C............E. Oliver

Exley, Jessie W., Leatherwood Lane, Wheeling, W. Va............A. Redmond

Farrell, Emily C., 106 Porter St., Easton, Pa.............................B. Mathews

Faucette, Mary K., Signal Mt., Chattanooga, Tenn.

Faulkner, Rosalie S., 1500 Madison St., Lynchburg, Va................S. Dunlap

Ferguson, Grace W., Merion, Pa...M. Copeland

Ferguson, M. Elizabeth, 138 Alabama St., Spartanburg, S. C.....S. Dodgen,
E. Crews, M. Timmerman, D. Fowler

Ferguson, Rachel B., 138 Alabama St., Spartanburg, S. C............R. Hendrix

Ferguson, R. Meredith, 345 Thrall Ave., Cincinnati, O.

Fishburne, Lucy L., Locust Grove, Charlottesville, Va........M. Edmondson

Foote, Sara K., 200 Prado, Atlanta, Ga............A. Porter, S. Southerland

Ford, Fanny P., 2717 Rivermont Ave., Lynchburg, Va................I. Moore

Foster, Elizabeth, Hotel Margaret, Brooklyn, N. Y...........................J. Kerr

Forsyth, Elizabeth, 2744 Hanover Circle, Birmingham, Ala...R. Manning,
E. Cates

Fowler, Dorothy E., 50 Beeching St., Worcester, Mass.. S. Dodgen, E. Crews,
M. Timmerman, E. Ferguson

Fuller, Darley K., 414 W. 121 St., New York City........................M. Lyon

Furman, Constance, 6 Broadus Ave., Greenville, S. C.

Gaines, Nancy E., 780 Riverside Drive, New York City................G. Olcott

Gall, Jean A., 417-23rd Ave. E., Duluth, Minn...................................E. Cox

Garland, Dorothy S., 88 Prospect Park West, Brooklyn, N. Y.......................
A. Eskesen, M. B. Green

Gates, Phyllis J., 501 W. Washington Ave., Jackson, Mich............A. Barber

Geer, Gratia F., 2553 Glenwood Ave., Toledo, O................H. M. Williams

Giese, Emilie I., 200 Lyncroft Rd., New Rochelle, N. Y................G. Prior

Giesecke, Claire M., 511 W. Russell Pl., San Antonio, Tex........E. Crenshaw

Gilchrist, A. Elsetta, 3022 W. 14th St., Cleveland, O.................J. Boone

Gochnauer, Anne F., Upperville, Va....................................N. L. Antrim

Gochnauer, Mary A., Shamrock, Charlottesville, Va....................J. Thomas

Gorsline, Elizabeth, 4006 Hermitage Rd., Richmond, Va............S. Meador

Graham, Katharyn J., 1919 E. 2nd St., Duluth, Minn...............G. Wilson

Gray, Frances M., 1714 Broadway, Little Rock, Ark...................E Copeland

Green, Janet B., 326 No. Grove St., Lock Haven, Pa.....R. Rich, N. Sherrill

Green, Margaret B., 28 Lenox Rd., Summit, N. J.....D. Garland, A. Eskesen

Green, Margaret F., 1924 Grove Ave., Richmond, Va................A. Babbitt

Gressitt, Margaret A., 4000 Maine Ave., Baltimore, Md....................A. Blake

Griffith, Margery I., 5th & Monroe Sts., Media, Pa................V. Le Hardy

Gubelman, Hallet, Woodland Ave., Englewood, N. J................M. Kneedler

Guigon, Elizabeth, 1125 W. Franklin St., Richmond, Va...E. Baker, M. Shelton

Hall, Anna L., 535 Chesterfield St., Aiken, S. C.....................E. Henderson

Hall, Margaret, 173 Lawn Ave., Stamford, Conn............................M. Diack

Halsey, Josephine E., 200 Smith St., Peekskill, N. Y...............D. Conaghan

Hanner, Claire D., 118 Linwood Ave., Atlanta, Ga....S. Jamison, T. Maybank

Harding, Margaret, 814 Macon Ave., Canon City, Colo.....H. Smyser, E. Neill

Harman, Ann C., Tazewell, Va.

Harms, Elizabeth W., 4614 Chester Ave., Philadelphia, Pa............M. Jayne

Harned, Louise I., 830 Mississippi Ave., Davenport, Iowa.........A. Sheppard

Harper, Louise, 35 St. Paul Rd., Ardmore, Pa.

Harpster, Hilda T., 2141 Robinwood Ave., Toledo, O...E. Bachman, E. Miller

Harrison, Frances M., 2525 E. 2nd St., Duluth, Minn................E. Marston

Harrold, Alice, 302 College St., Americus, Ga............................M. Taber

Hasson, Eliza R., 728 East End Ave., Pittsburgh, Pa............E. B. Williams

Heath, Rosa, 912 Westover Ave., Norfolk, Va............E. Wood, A. E. Moore

Henderson, Adelaide, Aiken, S. C.

Henderson, Eleanor, Aiken, S. C......................................A. S. Hall

Henderson, Jane, 2941 Newark St., Washington, D. C................R. Keeler

Hendon, Elizabeth, Hendersonville Rd., Asheville, N. C...............E. Jackson

Hendrix, Ruth, Piedmont Rd., Atlanta, Ga..............................R. Ferguson

Hibbs, Elizabeth F., 407 E. Northern Ave., Springfield, O...............K. Coe

Hiett, Margaret L., 2134 Parkwood Ave., Toledo, O....................H. Smith

Hix, Elizabeth J., Wise, Va...M. Lambeth

Hodgson, Virginia E., 268 E. 40th St., Norfolk, Va.

Hodnett, Margaret J., 629 Piedmont Ave., Atlanta, Ga.

Hoffman, Adaline, 1050 Lincoln Ave., Tyrone, Pa................M. M. Moore

Holderness, Anna S., Tarboro, N. C....................................L. Wood

Hollis, Amelia Fay, Bennettsville, S. C............................D. Paddock

Holt, Mary A., Clyde Court Apts., Miami, Fla.....................C. Manson

Horton, Charlotte F., 28 Easterly Ave., Auburn, N, Y...................M. Sumner

Howard, Frances E., 923 Larchmont Crescent, Norfolk, Va...................

E. Lankford, E. Tyler

Hoyt, Claire K., 6 Butler Pl., Garden City, L. I....................C. Woodward

Hughes, Mary Adelaide, 46 S. State Street, Dover, Delaware.........F. Brown

Humel, Dorothy F., 3223 Daisy Ave., Cleveland, O............M. L. Shidler

Huntington, Mary J., 709 N. Madison St., Rome, N. Y............W. Rankin

Hurlock, Elizabeth A., Cape Charles, Va..V. Davies

Irving, Beulah J., 26 Court St., Portsmouth, Va........................R. Young

Name	Address	Roommate

Jackson, Elizabeth K., 1105-18th Ave. S., Nashville, Tenn.

Jackson, Evelyn H., 365 Merrimon Ave., Asheville, N. C.............E. Hendon

Jackson, Katherine, 917 Oak St., Chattanooga, Tenn.

Jackson, Mercer L., 1105 18th Ave., Nashville, Tenn...................L. Miller

Jamison, Sarah L., 802 Providence Rd., Charlotte, N. C.........C. Hanner,
T. Maybank

Jayne, Marion I., 5721 Stanton Ave., Pittsburgh, Pa...................E. Harms

Jaspersen, Emily R., 124 So. Perry St., St. Marys, O.....................W. Springer

Johnson, Catherine C., J. G. Wilson Corp., Norfolk, Va....M. Meade,
V. Wilson

Johnstone, Alice W., 5312 Greenwood Ave., Chicago, Ill.............M. Curtis

Jolliffe, Dorothy E., 307 Rockwell Terrace, Frederick, Md.........M. Marshall

Jones, Alice L., 1088 Park Ave., New York City.......................A. J. Williams

Jones, Elizabeth W., 507 N. Taylor Ave., Kirkwood, Mo.............L. Bristol

Jones, Emily E., Chelsea St., Sistersville, W. Va.........D. Bunting, E. Dickinson

Keeler, Ruth, Meadow Brook Rd., Englewood, N. J................J. Henderson

Keen, Daisy S. 944 Main Street, Danville, Va............................E. Walthall

Kerr, Jean M., 692 Seward Ave., Detroit, Mich............................E. Foster

Kindleberger, Mattie L., 81 Maple Ave., Flushing, N. Y...........J. Callison

Kneedler, Margaret F., Garrett Ave., Swarthmore, Pa.............H. Gubelman

Kohler, Jane S., 102 E. 44th St., Savannah, Ga...............................M. New

Kohn, Eleanor J., 315 W. 71st St., New York City.....L. Conklin, E. Prescott
A. Newell

Kumm, Emily B., 8908 80th St., Union Course, L. I....................S. Doyle

Ladd, Mary V., 751 Franklin St., Clarksville, Tenn...................M. Lowder

Lamb, Isabel W., 236 S. Lexington Ave., White Plains, N. Y.........E. B. Sisson

Lambeth, Martha D., 2511 Kensington Pl., Nashville, Tenn.............E. Hix

LaNieve, Virginia, 1351 Carr Ave., Memphis, Tenn........................S. Massee

Lankford, Elizabeth C., 530 Shirley Ave., Norfolk, Va.....E. Tyler, F. Howard

Lawrence, Mary W. N., 627 Whitlock Ave., Marietta, Ga........M. C. Earle

Leadbeater, Katherine A., 414 N. Washington St., Alexandria, Va.

Lee, Janet N., 420 Park Ave., New York City

Lee, Mary L., Fernbank Ave., Cincinnati, O...............................L. Burks

LeHardy, Virginia, 110 Pelham Rd., Rochester, N. Y................M. Griffith

Leigh, Alice, 526 Shirley Ave., Norfolk, Va................................P. Soaper

Leigh, Margaret, 120 Sycamore St., Petersburg, Va.....E. Albers, E. B. Mathews

Leigh, Virginia L., 209 E. 15th St., Little Rock, Ark...................K. Little

Leonard, Mary B., 5223 Grand Ave., Birmingham, Ala.

Lewis, Anne, Amherst, Va.
Lewis, Barbara R., 186 Linwood Ave., Buffalo, N. Y.................M. Bronough
Lewis, Mildred E., Culpeper, Va.................................M. O. Speer
Little, Indel R., 3740 Military Rd., Chevy Chase, D. C............E. Shearman
Little, Katherine V., 501 N. 21st., Ft. Smith, Ark.........................V. Leigh
Lokey, Amanda B., 92 E. 14th St., Atlanta, Ga.................................N. Carnes
Lovett, Margaret W., "Gray Gables.," Huntington, W. Va.................P. Payne
Lowder, Margaret H., 1851 Dauphin Way, Mobile, Ala.................M. V. Ladd
Lowrance, Bess A., 400 N. 10th St., Ponca City, Okla.......J. Williamson
                     L. Stone, J. Watson
Lowrance, Ruth A., 400 N. 10th St., Ponca City, Okla.................M. Ambrose
Luck, Elizabeth A., Middleburg, Va.................................L. Collins
Lutz, Louise, 1629 Hyde Park Blvd., Chicago, Ill....................V. L. Campbell
Lyon, Mary D., 206 Windermere Ave., Wayne, Pa.........................D. Fuller
McCrady, Elizabeth F., 307 Maple Ave., Pittsburgh, Pa.................M. Stone
McDiarmid, Polly, 614 Evanswood Pl., Cincinnati, O....................F. Puckett
McGehee, Edna Earl, 3 Main St., Reidsville, N. C....................K. R. Smith
McIlroy, Lois, Irwin, Union Co., Ohio.
MacKain, Janet M., 378 Fairview Ave., Orange, N. J.
McKee, Sarah E., 428 Union Ave., Cranford, N. J.
MacVichie, Belle D., 702 E. S. Temple, Salt Lake City, Utah.
Macdonald, Mary E., 1503 Duncan Ave.; Chattanooga, Tenn.........M. Terrell
Macqueen, Millie, Katonah, N. Y.................................E. Cumnock
Mackoy, Margaret B., Lexington Pike, Covington, Ky...M. Weisiger, P. Roberts
Mahoney, Margaret D., 1422 Peachtree St., Atlanta, Ga.
Manning, Rebecca M., 369 E. Main St., Spartanburg, S. C.....E. Cates,
                     E. Forsyth
Manson, Clyde W., 729 Oak St., Chattanooga, Tenn.................M. A. Holt
Marks, Charlotte E., 201 Lexington Ave., Aspinwall, Pa.................L. Wooten
Marr, Katharine, 3325 Coliseum, New Orleans, La.................E. E. Clark
Marshall, Mary W., Leaksville, N. C.................................D. Jolliffe
Marshall, Myra St. J., 111 Middle St., Portsmouth, Va.........A. B. Winkelman
Marston, Elizabeth A., 2902 N. Calvert St., Baltimore, Md.........F. Harrison
Martindale, Carolyn V., 311 Park St., Oxford, Pa.
Massee, Sims, 104 Vineville Ave., Macon, Ga.............................V. La Neive
Mathews, Bonnie S., Plantation Mathews, La. (N. O.)...............E. Farrell
Mathews, Elizabeth B., 1501 Quarrier St., Charleston, W. Va.....E. Albers
                     M. Leigh

Name	*Address*	*Roommate*

Mathews, Helen C., 1700 Virginia St., Charleston, W. Va............E. Bruce

Maury, Caroline, 1141 Cherokee Rd., Louisville, Ky............E. P. Stevenson

Maupin, Martha W., 516 North St., Portsmouth, Va...................A. Torian

Maybank, Theodora P., 68 Meeting St., Charleston, S. C...C. Hanner, S. Jamison

Meade, Mary O., 139 S. Main St., Danville, Va............C. Johnson, V. Wilson

Meador, Sarah D., 2983 Peachtree Rd., Atlanta, Ga....................E. Gorsline

Meginnis, Dorothy P., 380 New Scotland Ave., Albany, N. Y.....M. V. Culver

Metz, Barbara B., Comfort Hill, Decatur, Ga...............................C. Brown

Miller, Lucy H., Oakwood Pl., Lynchburg, Va..........................M. Jackson

Miller, D. Elizabeth, 27 Walnut Ave., Wyoming, O...E. Bachman, H. Harpster

Moffett, Nancy, O., R. F. D. No. 2, Staunton, Va..............................J. Dillon

Moncure, Margaret T., P. O. Box 154, Richmond, Va........E. L. Valentine

Montague, Mary W., 2516 Monument Ave., Richmond, Va.....A. Ashhurst,
E. Councill, E. Clement

Moore, Anne E., Hotel Stonewall Jackson, Staunton, Va.....E. Wood, R. Heath

Moore, Frances E., 518 E. Main St., Rock Hill, S. C.

Moore, Ida B., 1620 Monument Ave., Richmond, Va....................F. P. Ford

Moore, Mary M., 3735 Paseo, Kansas City, Mo........................A. Hoffman

Morley, Elise L. Lone Pine Rd., Birmingham, Mich.

Moss, Mary L., 5220 Edgewater Drive, Norfolk, Va...............E. Thomason

Murphey, Merritt M., 2018 Wolfe St., Little Rock, Ark............E. Boone

Musgrave, Alice E., 307 N. William St., Goldsboro, N. C............T. Barksdale

Nash, Eugenia, 1425 Columbus Ave., Waco, Tex......................V. Plumb

Neal, Margaret E., Lucerne Court, Orlando, Fla............................S. Brooke

Neill, Elizabeth B., No. 1 Greendale Ave., Mt. Vernon, N. Y....H. Smyser,
M. Harding

Nelms, Mary B., 4532 Chestnut St., Philadelphia, Pa.

Nelson, Louise B., 1009 W. Franklin St., Richmond, Va...............A. Wilson

New, Margaret, 11016 Magnolia Drive, Cleveland, O...............J. Kohler

Newell, Anne L., 1 Clifton Rd., Atlanta, Ga....L. Conklin, E. Kohn,
E. Prescott

Nichols, Edwina G., 200 Fifth Ave., Denton, Md...............E. A. Cather

North, Isabelle W., 558 Greene St., Augusta, Ga............E. Tillman

Oakford, Helen M., 306 S. 15th St., St. Joseph, Mo...............D. Chambers

Olcott, Gwendolyn, 57 Fifth Ave., Nyack, N. Y......................N. Gaines

Oliver, Elizabeth W., 565 Greene St., Augusta, Ga...................S. Everett

Orr, Elizabeth R., 5708 Stanton Ave., Pittsburgh, Pa...............M. F. Clark

Orr, Gretchen, 1321 Michigan Ave., Cincinnati, O.

Owens, Katharine N., 2290 Calder Ave., Beaumont, Tex.....M. Brown,

E. Quisenberry, J. Snowdon

Paddock, Dorothea, 121 Raymond St., Cambridge, Mass..............A. Hollis

Parker, Mary F., 111 Astor St., Danville, Va................D. Snyder

Parsons, Katherine, 248 N. Edgeworth St., Greensboro, N. C.....M. V. Proctor

Patterson, Jessie J., 1501 Library Ave., McKeesport, Pa..............G. Wester

Patton, Anna, 911 E. Terrace, Chattanooga, Tenn.....E. Anderson, M. Chaffee

Payne, Pauline E., 233 Kevin Pl., Toledo, O...........................M. Lovett

Perkins, Alice Lee, 911 North St., Nacogdoches, Tex.

Perkins, Mary C., 125 Lorraine Ave., Upper Montclair, N. J.

Pernas, Christina P., 320 Prospect St., Cranford, N. J....................E. Robins

Phillips, Ella P., 909 Sumter St., Columbia, S. C...........................E. Ballard

Pickett, Mildred R., Madison, N. C..L. Young

Pleasants, Margaret J., 1006 Ritter Park, Huntington, W. Va.........V. Dey

Plumb, Vivian G., 140 Main St., Terryville, Conn.......................E. Nash

Poindexter, Daisye L., 1800 23rd Ave., Meridan, Miss...................A. Scott

Porter, Augusta T., 229 Prado, Atlanta, Ga............S. Foote, S. Southerland

Prentis, Lindsay, 703 Parker Ave., Detroit, Mich....................S. Ailes

Prescott, Elizabeth S., 206 W. Bloomfield St., Rome, N. Y..L. Conklin,

E. Kohn, A. Newell

Price, Anne Beth, 320 Army Blvd., San Antonio, Tex...................P. Bird

Prior, Gertrude, 29 Fisher Pl., Trenton, N. J......................E. Giese

Proctor, Mary V., 729 Quapaw Ave., Hot Springs, Ark...............K. Parsons

Puckett, Frances E., 640 6th Ave., Huntington, W. Va........P. McDiarmid

Quisenberry, Elva, 607 Felder Ave., Montgomery, Ala.....M. Brown,

J. Snowden, K. Owens

Rankin, Wilhelmina, 7 Stanley Oval, Westfield, N. J...........M. Huntington

Reahard, Mary E., 3339 Ruckle St., Indianapolis, Ind...............J. Saunders

Redmond, Alwyn A., 45 Beverly Rd., Ridgewood, N. J. ....J. Exley

Reed, Frances A., Knox Apts., Wheeling, W. Va...................E. Edmands

Reinvaldt, Christine V., 2050 Longfellow Ave., Detroit, Mich...D. Wrightnour

Rich, Robins M., Catonsville, Md..............................J. Green, N. Sherrill

Riddle, Jane D., 702 Holbrook Ave., Danville. Va........................C. Wailes

Riely, Emma C., 1524 Park Ave., Richmond, Va...................K. Eldridge

Robbins, Mary K., 911 Vermont Ave., Daytona, Fla.....C. Ellis, D. Wyckoff

Roberts, Polly M., 414 Conway St., Frankfort, Ky..M. Weisiger, M. Mackoy

Robins, Elizabeth H., 226 W. Lanvale St., Baltimore, Md............C. Pernas

Royer, Norvell E., Cary St., Richmond, Va...............................J. L. Baker

Ryan, Kathleen F., 19 Warfield St., Upper Montclair, N. J.........F. Cottman

Sanford, Mary M., Signal Mt., Tenn..M. Bromfield

Saunders, Jean, 364 Palisade Ave., Yonkers, N. Y....................M. E. Reahard

Saunders, Elizabeth, 1304 Farragut St., Washington, D. C............E. Williams

Scanlan, Elizabeth A., 903 Goodrich Ave., St. Paul, Minn.

Scott, Alice M., 1107 Charles St., Fredericksburg, Va............D. Pondexter

Shearman, Esther M., Levering Mill Rd., Cynwyd, Pa........................I. Little

Shelton, Mary E., 749 Vine St., Chattanooga, Tenn.....E. Baker, E. Guigon

Shepherd, Anne H., Washington Ave., Fredericksburg, Va............S. Dance

Shepherd, Mary L., 1812 E. Morehead St., Charlotte, N. C....M. Cucullu

Sheppard, L. Adela D., 938 W. 5th St., Winston-Salem, N. C.........L. Harned

Sherrill, Nancy W., 1205 15th St., Hickory, N. C............R. Rich, J. Green

Shidler, Mary L., 1013 E. Jefferson Blvd., So. Bend, Ind.............D. Humel

Shirley, Lucy, 3819 Seminary Ave., Richmond, Va.........................E. Wilson

Shortau, Florence K., 114 Second Ave., Little Falls, N. J.........N. W. Taylor,
                                                                          J. Warfield

Sisson, Eva B., Highwood Ave., Tenafly, N. J............................I. W. Lamb

Smith, Anna W., 29 Spears Ave., Asheville, N. C...............M. J. Abernethy

Smith, Elizabeth W., 601 Stanley Ave., E. W. H., Cincinnati, O.....M. Walker

Smith, Helen M., E. Palisade Ave., Englewood, N. J....................M. Hiett

Smith, Katherine R., 88 Tuscan Rd., Maplewood, N. J.........E. McGehee

Smyser, Helen F., 151 Roup St., Pittsburgh, Pa............E. Neill, M. Harding

Snowdon, Mary J., 2311 Conn. Ave., Washington, D. C........M. Brown,
                                                 E. Quisenberry, K. Owens

Snyder, Dorothy M., 2801 Wheeling St., El Paso, Tex........M. F. Parker

Soaper, Phoebe M., Harrodsburg, Ky...A. Leigh

Sollitt, Grace H., 3995 Ellis Ave., Chicago, Ill.

Southerland, Sarah H., 63 E. 17th., Atlanta, Ga................A. Porter, S. Foote

Speer, Mary O., 1118 N. 14th St., Ft. Smith, Ark.......................M. Lewis

Spingarn, Hope, Troutbeck, Amenia, N. Y.

Springer, Winogene, 724 Forest Ave., Wilmette, Ill..............E. Jaspersen

Stanbrough, Constance A., 1130 Parker Ave., Detroit, Mich.....A. Brent,
                                                 E. Duvall

Stephenson, Alice V., 2119 Hughitt Ave., Superior, Wis.

Stevenson, Elizabeth P., 311 S. 3rd Street, Wilmington, N. C.........C. Maury

Stone, E. Lucile, 15 Oakdale Rd., Atlanta, Ga.....J. Williamson, J. Watson,
                                                 B. Lowrance

Stone, Mildred C., 90 Pewabic St., Houghton, Mich...............E. McCrady

Name	*Address*	*Roommate*

Straus, Catharyn J., 1512 Beechwood Blvd., Pittsburgh, Pa...........M. Bernard

Sturges, Marjorie S., 81 Riverside Drive, Greenwich, Conn.........M. Carpenter

Sumner, Marion A., 303 Linden St., Rome, N. Y........................C. Horton

Sunderland, Grace N., Fair View Farm, Laurel, Md.........................W. West

Taber, Marion P., 1007 Bull St., Columbia, S. C......................A. Harrold

Taliaferro, Margaret P., 206 Park Ave., Charlotte, N, C.

Taylor, Lilla J., 230 Lakewood Blvd., Detroit, Mich.................D. Zartman

Taylor, Nar Warren, 1372 Vinton Ave., Memphis, Tenn.........F. Shortau,

J. Warfield

Terrell, Margaret E., 1019 E. Rio Grande St., El Paso, Tex.....M.Macdonald

Thomas, Julia A., Centreville, Md...M. Gochnauer

Thomason, Elizabeth, 10451 S. Seely Ave., Chicago, Ill.................M. Moss

Thompson, Con Overton, Franklin Rd., Nashville, Tenn............G. Bartels

Tillman, Eugenie P., Quitman, Ga..I. North

Timmerman, Margaret, Batesburg, S. C.....S. Dodgen, E. Crews, D. Fowler,

E. Ferguson

Torian, Anna G., 1802 Talbott Ave., Indianapolis, Ind................M. Maupin

Tucker, Susie R., 420 N. Blount St., Raleigh, N. C...................C. Whinery

Tyler, Esther M., 1115 5th Ave., Huntington, W. Va...E. Lankford, F. Howard

Valentine, Elizabeth L., 12 E. Franklin St., Richmond, Va............M. Moncure

Van Ness, Constance C., 159 Center Ave., Little Falls, N. J.

Vizard, Mary K., Mobile, Ala

Von Schilling, Sarah P., Hampton, Va...M. Eaton

Wailes, Cornelia L., Salisbury, Md...J. Riddle

Walker, Mary A., 2950 Newark St., Washington, D. C...........E. W. Smith

Walthall, Edith A., 1410 Montana St., El Paso, Tex...................D. Keen

Wampler, Adelaide B., 3216 Macomb St., N. W., Wash., D. C........F. Watters

Ware, Evelyn, Amherst, Va.

Warfield, Lida B., 1742 Park St., Jacksonville, Fla.....N. W. Taylor, F. Shortau

Warren, Edna P., 716 S. Delaware Ave., Tampa, Fla.

Watson, Jocelyn J., 2012 Cowden Ave., Memphis, Tenn.....J. Williamson,

S. Stone, B. Lowrance

Watters, Frances E., 421 William St., Rome, N. Y...................A. Wampler

Webb, Alice E., 103 Washington St., Cumberland, Md.

Weisiger, Margaret P., 823 Hinman Ave., Evanston, Ill.....P. Roberts,

M. Mackoy

Weissenburger, Charlotte F., Point Pleasant, W. Va.................H. Williamson

Weitzmann, Helen M., Mahwah, N. J...E. Blake

West, Winifred, 264 W. 15th St., Tulsa, Okla........................G. Sunderland

Name	Address	Roommate

Wester, Gladys M., 63 Whittlesey Ave., East Orange, N. J.........J. Patterson

Whaley, Katharyn W., 370 College St., Macon, Ga....................L. Chapman

Whelan, Ruth M., 661 Seward Ave., Detroit, Mich.

Whinery, Charlotte T., 2044 Robinwood Ave., Toledo., O................S. Tucker

Wilkinson, Elizabeth S., Georgia Ave., Winston-Salem, N. C.....E. Dillard

Wilkinson, Jane E., Little Silver, N. J...J. Bruce

Williams, Alberta J., 701 Pingree Ave., Detroit, Mich................A. Jones

Williams, Catherine B., 1010 Graydon Ave., Norfolk, Va............M. B. Daily

Williams, Eleanor B., 308 Maple St., Danvers, Mass....................E. Hasson

Williams, Elizabeth, 6105 Howe St., Pittsburgh, Pa....................E. Saunders

Williams, Harriett M., 1100 Pickwick Ave., Springfield, Mo..........G. Geer

Williams, Huldah J., 606 W. Grace St., Richmond, Va..............A. Woodward

Williams, Margaret H., Scarsdale, N. Y.

Williamson, Hallie I., Fayetteville, N. C.....................C. Weissenburger

Williamson, Jean R., 48 So. McLean Bvld., Memphis, Tenn....J. Watson,

B. Lowrance, L. Stone

Wilson, Amelia S., Lookout Mt., Tenn...L. Nelson

Wilson, Eleanor, 1620 Niles Ave., St. Joseph, Mich.........................L. Shirley

Wilson, Georgia N., 403 Tazewell Ave., Cape Charles, Va........K. Graham

Wilson, Julia A., Lookout Mt., Tenn...L. L. Wood

Wilson, Mildred T., 834 Westover Ave., Norfolk, Va............J. R. Brown

Wilson, Virginia A., 403 Tazewell Ave., Cape Charles, Va.....C. Johnson,

M. Meade

Winkelman, Arra B., 267 S. Belvidere Blvd., Memphis, Tenn..M. Marshall

Wood, Elizabeth B., Edenton, N. C....................A. E. Moore, R. Heath

Wood, Lillian L., 2707 Monument Ave., Richmond, Va............J. Wilson

Wood, Lillian, 329 Kendal Pl., Columbus, O............................A. Holderness

Wood, Martha, 2933 N. Meridian St., Indianapolis, Ind.

Woodward, Amelia P., 918 Floyd Ave., Richmond, Va............H. Williams

Woodward, Cecil, Box 136, Sta. D., New York, N. Y....................C. Hoyt

Woodworth, Mary C., 608 E. Armour Blvd., Kansas City, Mo.........C. Clausen

Wooten, Charlotte L., 616 Miller St., Helena, Ark......................C. Marks

Wrightnour, Dorothy, 933 Woodlawn St., Scranton, Pa..........C. Reinvaldt

Wyckoff, Dorothy E., 225 Altamont Pl., Somerville, N. J.....M. K. Robbins,

C. Ellis

Young, Lillian E., 811 Jackson St., Corinth, Miss....................M. Pickett

Young, Rachel L., 75 Coit St., New London, Conn....................B. Irving

Zartman, Dorothy J., 1875 Roxbury Rd., Columbus, O................L. Taylor

CPSIA information can be obtained
at www.ICGtesting.com
Printed in the USA
BVHW040134141218
535545BV00018BA/1055/P

9 780656 592654